PIECE OF POETRY

ANVI KAKRIA

ISBN 979-888521937-2

Contents

1. IT'S TIME TO SMILE!!

IT'S TIME TO SMILE

ITS TIME TO GIGGLE

LET'S COME AND CUDDLE

LET'S GO TO THE HAPPINESS WORLD AND MAKE IT MORE HAPPIER

HAPPINESS IS IMPERATIVE .SO DON'T WAIT FOR OTHERS

THE CHAIN START'S WITH YOU

SO YOU NEED TO HURRY UP!!

2. MY HEROS ARE MY PARENTS

THANK YOU MOM

THANK YOU DAD

THESE ARE SO SMALL WORDS

THERE ARE SO MUCH TO ADD

THERE ARE HEROS IN MY LIFE

THERE ARE HEROS IN MY HOME

THE HEROS CAN'T FLY BUT THE HEROS ARE SPECIAL

MY HEROS ARE BRAVE

• 4 •

MT HEROS ARE WARM

MY HEROS ARE MY EVERYTHING

AND MY HEROS ARE MY PARENTS!!

3. SNOWMAN

I MADE MY- SELF A SNOWMAN

AS PERFET AS IT COULD BE

I THOUGHT I'D KEEP IT AS A PET

AND LET IT SLEEP WITH ME

I MADE IT SOME PAJAMAS

AND PILLOW FOR ITS HEAD

THEN LAST NIGHT IT RAN AWAY

BUT FIRST IT WET THE BED!

• 6 •

4. BIRTHDAYS..

COUNT YOUR GARDEN WITH FLOWERS

NEVER BY THE LEAVES THAT FALL.

COUNT YOUR DAYS WITH GOLDEN HOURS

DONT REMEBER THE CLOUDS AT ALL.

COUNT YOUR NIGHTS WITH STARS NOT

BY SHADOWS.

COUNT YOUR LIFE WITH SMILES

NOT WITH TEARS.

5. ALWAYS TRY YOUR BEST

ALWAYS TRY YOUR BEST

NEVER LEAVE THE HOPE

IF YOU ALWAYS TRY YOUR BEST

THEN YOU NEVER HAVE TO WONDER

ABOUT WHAT YOU HAVE DONE

IF YOU SUMMONED YOUR THUNDER.

6. TEACHER

THANK FOR BEING MY TEACHER I SAY IT

WITH A PRIDE

THANKS FOR TAKING YOUR TIME

TO TEACH ME AS YOU HAVE DONE

YOU MADE LEARNING MORE INTRESTING

YOU MADE LEARNING MORE FUN

YOU GIVE YOUR TIME TO HELP US

PREPARE US FOR THE WORLD THAT IS OUTSIDE

THANK YOU FOR BEING MY TEACHER

I SAY IT WITH A PRIDE.